LOVE ON CONDITIONS

Stories of Understandable Communication in Marriage

Jennifer M. Reid-Walker

Certified Life Coach
www.Jmreidwalker.com

DAYELight
PUBLISHERS

ISBN: 978-1-958443-86-6 (paperback)

Dedication

This is dedicated to my children, who support me in all I do—Oshane, Zhavier, Daniel, and Matthew. I love you with all my heart.

To all the marriages that will be affected positively by these words, I thank God for the vision He gave me in my deepest, darkest moment when all I had was Him.

Endorsements

"I love the way she breaks down things that we do in our marriage that we are unaware of."

—**Tirell and Heather Bartell**

"I enjoyed reading this so much that I didn't want it to end! It is clear that this is your passion/calling. I love each scenario depicting the profoundness of each gem. This is reality, and many marriages will benefit from this."

—**Arlene Wright**

"It was a great event and such a kind speaker. Very knowledgeable and easy to talk to."

—**Jaye and Ashley Grant**

Acknowledgments and Introduction

With gratitude to those who believed in me and have allowed me to assist them over the years with kind words and a shoulder to lean on.

It was in my darkest moments of navigating a failing marriage that the Holy Ghost visited me with a vision and a charge to assist those who are at the brink of letting go of the meaning of their vows and dedication. In navigating this charge, I learned that marriages are failing because couples simply do not understand each other and have given up on the patience and compromise it takes to succeed in a relationship.

These are short stories of incidents in marriages and how couples traverse their journeys to a positive and fruitful end.

LOVE ON CONDITIONS

Stories of Understandable Communication in Marriage

Table of Contents

Chapter One

Some Things Are Taught, And Some Things Are Caught

We all are brought up with values, beliefs, and attitudes in our family dynamics; however, there are other behaviors that we gravitate to outside of the home that we use to navigate life.

Michael grew up in a bustling household with five siblings—two brothers and three sisters. Though not devoutly religious, his parents had instilled in their children a deep sense of spirituality. The family didn't attend church regularly, but they observed certain rituals that were ingrained in their daily lives. Prayers before meals, bed, and any significant task were non-negotiable.

Michael's father rarely attended church, showing up only for weddings and funerals, while his mother made appearances at special events like Christmas services or Easter celebrations. Despite their parents' sporadic church attendance, the children were expected to be in church every Sunday, learning and living by Christian principles.

As a child, Michael followed these teachings diligently. He prayed before bed, meals, and important moments. However, as he grew older and entered adulthood, he began to question these rituals. Life presented new challenges and influences, and Michael found himself

> Despite their parents' sporadic church attendance, the children were expected to be in church every Sunday, learning and living by Christian principles.

straying from the strict religious practices of his upbringing. He stopped attending church regularly and only prayed before bed when he felt troubled. Yet, one habit stuck with him—praying before meals. It was a small ritual he couldn't let go of.

He once shared a story with friends about a potluck at his office where everyone except him fell ill after eating the fish. Michael believed it was because he had prayed over his food, a habit he had never abandoned. This event reinforced his belief in the power of prayer and highlighted the contrast between his upbringing and the life he was living. He noticed that many of his friends didn't observe the same rituals or hold the same beliefs, yet they seemed to navigate life just fine. This realization made him question the necessity of some of the practices he had grown up with. He began to slack off, adopting a more relaxed approach to his faith and lifestyle.

Joanne entered Michael's life during this period of self-discovery. Her background was starkly different from Michael's. Joanne and her sister were raised in a broken home with divorced parents who had little interest in religious or spiritual practices. Joanne's childhood was marked by instability, moving between her mother's house during the week and her father's on weekends and holidays. Religion had no place in their home; there were no prayers, church services, or discussions about faith. Instead, her parents smoked, drank, and frequently fought, using words as weapons in their ongoing battles.

Despite the chaotic environment, Joanne and her sister remained close. They had developed their own rituals of love and support, always greeting each other with hugs and kisses and never parting without saying, "I love you." This bond was their sanctuary, a stark contrast to the volatility around them.

When Michael and Joanne got married, they brought their vastly different backgrounds into their new life together. Raising their own children, they were faced with the challenge of blending their upbringings into a cohesive family dynamic. Michael, though less strict about his religious practices than his parents, still valued the rituals he had grown up with. On the other hand, Joanne had never experienced a structured religious environment, but she cherished the warmth and affection she shared with her sister.

Together, Michael and Joanne embarked on creating a family that reflected the best of both worlds. They decided to take what they valued from their respective upbringings and discard what didn't serve them.

Michael's love for prayer and religious rituals found a place in their home, but it was balanced with the warmth and emotional openness that Joanne brought from her childhood.

They agreed that going to church as a family was important, not because of strict adherence to religious doctrine, but as a way to instill a sense of community and moral grounding in their children. They introduced the practice of praying together—not just before meals but also during moments of need or gratitude. Prayer became a way for them to connect as a family, to share their hopes, fears, and thanks.

At the same time, they embraced Joanne's practice of expressing love openly and frequently. Their home was filled with hugs, kisses, and the words "I love you." They wanted their children to grow up in an environment where affection was freely given and received, where emotional expression was encouraged rather than suppressed.

In addition to the traditions from their childhoods, Michael and Joanne were open to learning from the world around them. They read books on parenting, watched shows that offered insights into family dynamics, and listened to podcasts that discussed modern approaches to raising children. They weren't afraid to adapt and evolve, incorporating new ideas that resonated with their values.

Over time, they crafted a family life that felt right for them. It was a blend of the spiritual and the emotional, the traditional and the modern. They discarded the aspects of their upbringings that felt burdensome or outdated and kept what felt meaningful. For Michael, this meant maintaining a connection to his faith but without the rigidity of his childhood. For Joanne, it meant creating a home filled with love and warmth, a refuge from the coldness she had experienced as a child.

> Over time, they crafted a family life that felt right for them. It was a blend of the spiritual and the emotional, the traditional and the modern.

As they watched their children grow, Michael and Joanne felt confident that they were doing their best to create a family dynamic that was both nurturing and grounding. They had taken the values, beliefs, and attitudes they were raised with and combined them with the behaviors they had gravitated toward as adults. In doing so, they built a home that was uniquely theirs—a place where faith and love coexisted, where prayers were said and hugs were given freely, and where their children could grow up feeling secure and cherished.

They used the things they were taught and what they caught along the way to build their family. They now have a family dynamic that they are comfortable with and think that they are doing the best for their family.

"Train up a child in the way he should go, and when he is old he will not depart from it." (Proverbs 22:6 – NKJV).

Chapter Two

Don't Let Your Spouse Leave the Room

Not getting validation from your spouse, not getting a compliment, or not verbally communicating with your spouse can lead to a breakdown in your relationship.

Robert and Jill had been married for twenty years, a milestone many couples never reach. Together, they had built a life that, on the surface, seemed enviable. They had two beautiful daughters, Emily and Sarah, who were now away at college. The house that once echoed with laughter and the noise of a bustling family was now quiet, and the emptiness was palpable. Robert and Jill had entered a new phase of their lives—empty nesters. But instead of finding comfort in each other, they drifted apart, the distance between them growing wider with each passing year.

It wasn't always this way. There was a time when they couldn't get enough of each other, and the thought of being apart was unbearable. But life had a way of creeping in with its endless demands and responsibilities. Robert had thrown himself into his career, climbing the corporate ladder with the same determination that had once fueled his passion for Jill. Jill, too, had dedicated herself to her work, finding fulfillment in her role as a project manager at a large tech firm. Raising their daughters and managing their careers left little time for each other, and slowly but surely, the connection they once cherished began to fray.

At first, it was subtle—missed conversations, forgotten dates, and the lack of simple gestures that once came so naturally. Compliments, once freely given, became rare. The words "You look beautiful" or "I'm proud of you" were replaced with silence. Robert and Jill stopped noticing the little things that made their relationship special. They were no longer each other's confidants or cheerleaders; instead, they became roommates, coexisting in the same space but living separate lives.

As the years went by, the chasm between Robert and Jill grew. The once solid foundation of their marriage began to crack, and they found themselves seeking solace elsewhere. Robert met Lisa, a colleague at his firm who always had a kind word or a compliment for him. She noticed the little things—his new tie, how he handled a difficult client, the effort he put into his work. Lisa made him feel valued in a way that Jill hadn't in years.

> The once solid foundation of their marriage began to crack, and they found themselves seeking solace elsewhere.

Jill, too, found herself drawn to someone else; Mark, a senior executive at her company, who seemed attentive and thoughtful. He would bring her coffee in the mornings, compliment her on her achievements, and listen to her frustrations. Jill felt seen and appreciated with Mark, something she hadn't felt with Robert in a long time.

Neither Robert nor Jill set out to have an affair, but the emotional void they felt in their marriage made them vulnerable. The attention and validation they received from Lisa and Mark filled a need that had gone unmet for years. The affairs were not just about physical attraction but about feeling valued, respected, and wanted. For Robert and Jill, the validation they craved came in the form of compliments and attention—something they no longer received from each other.

The affairs continued for months, with Robert and Jill both keeping their secrets. But the guilt weighed heavily on them. They knew what they were doing was wrong, but the validation they received from their respective partners was intoxicating. However, the illusion of happiness began to crumble when their daughters came home for a visit during a holiday break.

Emily and Sarah immediately noticed the tension between their parents. The once warm and loving home now felt cold and distant. The girls confronted their parents, asking them what had happened to the happy couple they had always known. It was then that Robert and Jill were forced to confront the reality of their situation.

They realized they had become strangers to each other, not because of the affairs, but because they had stopped communicating. They had stopped validating each other, offering compliments, and being there for one another. The affairs were a symptom of a much deeper issue—the lack of emotional intimacy and connection in their marriage.

After the girls returned to college, Robert and Jill were again left alone in their quiet house. But this time, the silence was suffocating. They knew they couldn't continue living this way, pretending everything was

> They realized they had become strangers to each other, not because of the affairs, but because they had stopped communicating.

fine when it was anything but. One evening, Robert finally broke the silence.

"We need to talk," he said, his voice heavy with emotion.

Jill nodded, knowing that this conversation was long overdue. They sat down at the kitchen table, the same table where they had shared countless meals and conversations over the years. But tonight, it felt different.

"I've been having an affair," Robert admitted, his voice barely above a whisper.

Jill's heart sank, but she wasn't surprised. She had known deep down that something was wrong. "So have I," she confessed, tears welling up in her eyes.

The weight of their confessions hung in the air, and for a moment, neither of them knew what to say. But then, something shifted. Instead of anger or blame, they felt a deep sense of sadness—for the marriage they had neglected, for the love they had lost, and for the people they had become.

"Why did we let it get this far?" Jill asked, her voice trembling.

Robert shook his head, unable to find an answer. "I don't know. I guess we stopped caring and stopped trying. We took each other for granted."

Jill nodded, wiping away her tears. "I think we both just wanted to feel appreciated and we found that in other people because we weren't giving it to each other." Robert and Jill had allowed each other to "leave the room," so the relationship was bent.

In order to "Always have your spouse in the room," here are a couple of scenarios:

Wrong Way

Co-worker: Hi, Jill. I love to see you in that dress/or that dress looks good on you.

Jill: *(blushing)* Thank you.

Getting a compliment from someone when you are not getting it from your spouse can—and will—have you veering towards what you want to hear, so in the long run, you may get close to someone who gives you the attention that you need, and before you know it, you start an extra-marital affair.

Try this:

Right Way

Co-worker: Hi, Jill. I love to see you in that dress/or that dress looks good on you.

Jill: You know, that is exactly what my husband told me this morning. Thank you.

When it is done that way, Jill now brings Robert into the room, and with that, there is a barrier or protection that will show that she is involved with someone and there is no space for another person. This can be done to protect your marriage. Your spouse may have complimented you at some other time, or because you are married, you should be intentional about protecting your marriage and building a hedge around it.

The road to healing was not easy. Robert and Jill knew they had a long way to go if they wanted to rebuild their marriage. They sought counseling, not just to address the affairs but to understand why they had grown apart in the first place. Through therapy, they learned about the importance of communication, validation, and appreciation in their relationship.

They made a commitment to each other to start afresh and put in the effort they had once taken for granted. They began complimenting each other again, noticing the little things, and expressing their love and appreciation. It wasn't easy—there were days when the pain and resentment threatened to overwhelm them—but they pushed through, determined to make their marriage work.

Slowly, the connection they had lost began to return. They started spending more time together, going on dates, and rediscovering the things they loved about each other. They learned that a successful marriage wasn't just about love but effort, communication, and the willingness to grow together.

As the years passed, Robert and Jill found themselves in a new chapter of their lives. They were no longer the same people they were when they first got married, but they had grown stronger together. Their marriage was not perfect—no marriage ever is—but it was real and worth fighting for.

In the end, Robert and Jill learned that validation and compliments were not just nice-to-haves in a relationship; they were essential. They realized that by neglecting these small but significant acts, they had allowed their marriage to deteriorate. But by making the conscious decision to be there for each other and offer words of affirmation and love, they were able to rebuild their relationship and find their way back to each other.

"And be kind to one another, tenderhearted, forgiving one another, even as God in Christ forgave you." (Ephesians 4:32 – NKJV).

Chapter Three

Smile at the Bulldog

In a world of chaos, heartaches, unforgiveness, and pain, we will say to ourselves, "Life is not fair," and it is true because if life was fair, it would not be L.I.F.E. but F.A.I.R., so as we navigate this life, we need to learn that everyone has issues and is dealing with something. We need to be gentle with each other as well as ourselves. A person may have a sad or angry face, and if you try to match up to them with their looks and attitude, you will end up hurting yourself because if

> "Life is not fair," and it is true because if life was fair, it would not be L.I.F.E. but F.A.I.R.

you are a happy person, you will be stepping out of your comfort zone to please someone else and that will only hurt you.

Jan and Samuel's love story began on a sunny afternoon during a church singles retreat. It was a weekend meant for spiritual growth, connection, and reflection, but for Jan and Samuel, it became the starting point of something far deeper. Jan, with her bright smile and infectious energy, was the life of the group, effortlessly making friends and spreading laughter wherever she went. On the other hand, Samuel was reserved, observing the lively group from a distance. He was there for spiritual enrichment, not socializing, and certainly not for finding romance.

Yet, fate had other plans. During a group activity that required pairing up, Jan found herself partnered with Samuel. She approached him with her usual enthusiasm, introducing herself with a wide grin. "Hi, I'm Jan. Looks like we're partners in this adventure."

Samuel nodded politely, offering a reserved smile. "Samuel. Nice to meet you."

Jan's bubbly personality began to chip away at Samuel's guarded exterior as they worked together. She cracked jokes, made light of their mistakes, and approached the task with a carefree attitude that was foreign to Samuel.

He found himself both fascinated and bewildered by her. By the end of the day, Samuel was surprised to find that he had actually enjoyed himself, largely due to Jan's influence.

Over the course of the retreat, Jan and Samuel spent more time together. Their conversations deepened, revealing shared values, interests, and a mutual attraction. Despite their contrasting personalities, there was an undeniable connection between them. By the end of the weekend, they were inseparable, and within months, they were officially a couple.

Jan and Samuel reveled in the thrill of new love for the first year of their relationship. They complemented each other in ways neither of them had expected. Jan brought laughter and lightness into Samuel's life, helping him to relax and enjoy the little things. Samuel, in turn, provided Jan with stability and grounded her when her happy-go-lucky nature threatened to lead her astray.

But as the initial excitement began to fade, their differences became more pronounced. Jan's spontaneous, carefree attitude sometimes clashed with

Samuel's serious, methodical approach to life. While Jan saw the world as a playground full of possibilities, Samuel viewed it through a lens of caution and responsibility.

One evening, as they were planning their wedding, these differences came to a head. Full of excitement, Jan suggested a whimsical theme for their big day—a colorful, garden-style wedding with quirky decorations and playful elements. Samuel, ever the pragmatist, frowned at the idea.

"Jan, a wedding is a serious occasion. It's not a time for frivolity. We should keep it simple and elegant," Samuel argued, his tone firm.

Jan's smile faded as she realized how differently they viewed the event. "But, Samuel, it's our wedding, it should be a reflection of us, of our love and our personalities. It doesn't have to be boring."

Samuel sighed, sensing the tension rising between them. "It's not about being boring, Jan. It's about setting the right tone. We need to think about the future, about how we'll look back on this day."

The conversation ended with both of them feeling frustrated and misunderstood. It wasn't the first time their differing perspectives had caused friction, but it felt more significant this time. They loved each other deeply but were beginning to realize that love alone wasn't enough to smooth over the cracks in their relationship.

Jan and Samuel found themselves increasingly at odds as their wedding day approached. They had heated discussions about everything from the guest list to the honeymoon destination. Each disagreement highlighted their contrasting personalities—Jan's desire for spontaneity and fun clashed with Samuel's need for order and tradition.

Despite these challenges, they both knew they didn't want to lose each other. They had invested two years into their relationship, and their love was real. However, they also recognized that they needed to find a way to reconcile their differences if they wanted their marriage to succeed.

One evening, after yet another disagreement, Samuel suggested they seek counsel from their pastor, who had been a guiding force in their lives. Jan agreed, hoping that an outside perspective could help them find common ground.

The pastor listened patiently during their session as Jan and Samuel expressed their frustrations and concerns. After a thoughtful pause, he spoke gently. "It's clear that you both love each other very much, but love isn't just about enjoying the good times. It's about working through the challenges together, finding compromise, and understanding that your differences can be strengths, not weaknesses."

He turned to Jan. "Jan, your joy and spontaneity are gifts. They bring light into Samuel's life and remind him to enjoy the journey. But Samuel's seriousness and focus are also gifts. They provide stability and direction, helping you both stay on track."

The pastor then looked at Samuel. "Samuel, it's important to recognize that Jan's approach to life doesn't undermine your values. Instead, it complements them. And Jan, Samuel's caution isn't meant to stifle your spirit but to protect and guide you both."

He encouraged them to find ways to balance their personalities, to compromise where necessary, and to always communicate openly. "Marriage is a partnership," he reminded them. "It's not about winning or losing arguments, but about finding a path that works for both of you."

With the pastor's guidance, Jan and Samuel began to approach their relationship differently. They realized they needed to embrace each other's differences rather than see them as obstacles. Jan started to appreciate Samuel's careful planning and attention to detail, recognizing that it brought structure to their lives. Samuel, in turn, learned to let go a little, allowing himself to enjoy the spontaneous moments that Jan cherished.

They revisited their wedding plans with a new mindset, blending their ideas into a celebration that reflected both of their personalities. The result was a beautiful, elegant garden wedding that had touches of whimsy and fun, just as Jan had envisioned, but with the understated sophistication that Samuel valued.

Their relationship was far from perfect, but they were learning to navigate their differences with grace and understanding. They had discovered that their contrasting personalities didn't have to be a source of conflict; instead, they could be a source of strength. By embracing what made each of them unique, they found a way to create a life together that was richer and more balanced than either of them could have imagined.

> They had discovered that their contrasting personalities didn't have to be a source of conflict; instead, they could be a source of strength.

The bulldog was born with a face that is filled with creases and folds, so there is nothing that that type of dog can do to change its look or else it will hurt itself. In the same breath, if someone does not have your personality or beliefs and you try to change yourself to be like them, in the end, you will only be hurting yourself and may even lose yourself, so it is best to smile at the bulldogs in your life.

As Jan and Samuel stood together on their wedding day, surrounded by family and friends, they knew that their journey was just beginning. There would be challenges ahead, but they felt ready to face them together. Their love had been tested, but it had also been strengthened. At that moment, they realized that their differences were not a weakness but a testament to the depth and resilience of their love.

They had learned that in the dance of marriage, it wasn't about leading or following but about finding a rhythm that allowed them both to shine. And as they looked into each other's eyes, they knew they had found that rhythm, a harmony that would carry them through the rest of their lives.

"Let your gentleness be known to all men. The Lord *is* at hand. Be anxious for nothing, but in everything by prayer and supplication, with thanksgiving, let your requests be made known to God; and the peace of God, which surpasses all understanding, will guard your hearts and minds through Christ Jesus." (Philippians 4:5-7 – NKJV).

Chapter Four

Be Gentle With Your Heart

The Bent's marriage of thirty-five years was admired by everyone in their small community. With three grown children and three beautiful granddaughters, they were seen as the epitome of a happy family. Mrs. Bent was deeply committed to her faith, serving as a Missionary and Greeter at her church, while Mr. Bent, though not as devout, supports her by attending church occasionally. They were self-employed, with Mr. Bent running a car wash business and Mrs. Bent operating a food truck. Despite their busy lives, they always found time to share a home-cooked meal every evening, a ritual that solidified their bond.

While the Bents continued to be the model couple in their community, unseen cracks began to form in their marriage. Mr. Bent became increasingly distant, and

Mrs. Bent, absorbed in her faith and responsibilities, failed to notice the growing gap between them. One day, Mr. Bent made a choice that would shatter the peace of their lives—he began an affair with one of his employees. As the months pass, the affair became more serious, and Mrs. Bent remained blissfully unaware, believing in the strength of their marriage and the love they have always shared.

The truth eventually came out, and Mrs. Bent was devastated by the betrayal. Her world was turned upside down, but her faith guided her response. Instead of reacting with anger or bitterness, she chose the path of forgiveness, a decision rooted in her Christian principles. She was determined to save her marriage and repair the damage done, even though the pain cut deep. Mr. Bent, filled with guilt and shame, ended the affair and attempted to mend the rift between them. The road to healing was long, but Mrs. Bent remained steadfast in her commitment to her vows.

Years passed, and life began to resemble a new normal. The couple found a rhythm again, but the wounds from the first betrayal had not fully healed. When Mr. Bent strayed again, this time moving out to live with his mistress, Mrs. Bent was left shattered. The weight of the second betrayal was almost too much to bear, and she sank into a deep depression. Friends and family urged her to be kind to herself and to protect her heart, but the pain was overwhelming. She lost weight and withdrew from the world, but her faith never wavered, even in the darkest of times.

> Her love for him had never truly faded, and his return eased the loneliness she had felt.

During the four years that Mr. Bent lived with his mistress, Mrs. Bent slowly began to heal. She found solace in her church community and in the love of her children and grandchildren. The process was slow, but she started to regain her physical and emotional strength. She learned to live without her husband, to find joy in small moments, and to take care of herself. Despite everything, she continued to pray for her husband, hoping that one day he would return to the man she once knew.

Unexpectedly, after four years, Mr. Bent returned home. He realized the error of his ways and was filled with regret. Mrs. Bent, despite all the pain he had caused, welcomed him back with open arms. Her love for him had never truly faded, and his return eased the loneliness she had felt. Mr. Bent was a changed man, humbled by his experiences and aware of the damage he had done. He sought redemption and found it in the same faith that had sustained his wife. He gave his life to the Lord, was baptized, and became an active member of her church, striving to be the husband she deserved.

Just as the Bents began to rebuild their lives together, Mr. Bent suffered a stroke. The illness left him weakened, and Mrs. Bent stepped into the role of caretaker with the same devotion she had shown throughout their marriage. Despite everything, she cared for him with love and tenderness, never allowing the past to cloud her commitment to him. Even when he suffered another stroke, losing movement on his left side, she remained at his side, her love unwavering. For seven years, she dedicated herself to his care, showing the true strength of her character and the depth of her love.

The final years of Mr. Bent's life were marked by the gentle care of his wife. Though his body failed him, he found peace in the love and forgiveness of the woman he once took for granted. Mrs. Bent's faith remained her guiding light, and she took solace in knowing that she had fulfilled her vows in every sense. When Mr. Bent passed away, she mourned deeply but was comforted by the knowledge that they had found their way back to each other. Her strength and devotion were recognized by all who knew them, and she was left with the memories of a love that, despite its trials, endured to the end.

"Above all, guard your heart, for everything you do flows from it." (Proverbs 4:23 – NIV).

Chapter Five

Next Year This Time

Raymond and Rose were known among their friends and family as the embodiment of a perfect couple. Their love was a subject of admiration and envy; they seemed to understand each other in ways that others could only dream of. They shared similar tastes, ambitions, and an unshakeable bond, making their relationship seem effortless. The couple often bragged about how their compatibility made loving each other a breeze.

Then came the pandemic. The world turned upside down, and Raymond and Rose, like many others, found themselves suddenly unemployed. The vibrant life they had enjoyed began to crumble under the weight of financial strain and uncertainty. The stress of their new reality began seeping into their relationship, revealing previously hidden cracks.

As the weeks turned into months, the pressure of their diminished financial resources took its toll. The couple found themselves arguing over things they had never disputed before. Small annoyances grew into larger conflicts, and the comfort of their home seemed to turn into a battleground. Despite their love, they found it increasingly difficult to maintain the harmony they once had.

One evening, as they sat across from each other at their cramped dining table, Raymond and Rose had an epiphany. They realized they had been focusing too much on their differences rather than their shared strengths, and this moment of clarity prompted them to confront their problems head-on and communicate more openly about their fears and frustrations.

Determined to navigate this challenging period together, Raymond and Rose made a plan. They began by cutting unnecessary expenses, prioritizing their needs, and seeking new income opportunities. They took on freelance jobs, sold items they no longer needed, and even started a small online business. Their financial situation began to stabilize, and their relationship improved.

Each small victory, whether it was finding a new client or successfully budgeting for the month, became a source of renewed hope for Raymond and Rose. They celebrated these wins together, finding joy in the little things. Their bond strengthened as they worked together towards their shared goals, rediscovering the partnership that had once been their strength.

Despite their efforts, not everything went smoothly. They faced setbacks, including unexpected expenses and periods of intense stress. They reminded themselves of their shared belief during these times: "Next year, this time, things will be different." This mantra became their source of motivation and resilience, helping them push through the tough moments.

> Despite their efforts, not everything went smoothly. They faced setbacks, including unexpected expenses and periods of intense stress.

Through their trials, Raymond and Rose began to reconnect on a deeper level. They made time for each other amidst their busy schedules, rediscovering the simple pleasures of their relationship. They engaged in activities they had enjoyed before, like cooking together and long walks in the park. Their love, once tested, grew stronger and more meaningful.

As the year drew to a close, Raymond and Rose found themselves in a much better place. Their financial situation had improved, and they had adapted to their new normal. They survived and thrived, transforming their hardship into a testament to their enduring love and commitment. They looked back on their journey with pride, grateful for the lessons learned and the strength gained.

With renewed hope and a stronger relationship, Raymond and Rose embraced the future with optimism. They continued building on their successes, knowing they could face any challenge together. As they looked ahead, they were confident that "next year, this time" would bring even greater joys and achievements. Their love story, once tested by adversity, now stood as a beacon of resilience and enduring connection.

"There is one body and one spirit, just as you were called in one hope of your calling." (Ephesians 4:4 – NKJV).

Author bio

Jennifer Reid-Walker is a life coach and author from Clayton, North Carolina, who specializes in the dynamics of communication within marriages. She has worked in People Relations for over thirty years and is an immigrant from the island of Jamaica. She has many years of experience as a motivational speaker, transformational coach, and mentor and has dedicated her career to helping couples build deeper, emotional connections through clear, compassionate, and effective communication.

Jennifer is more than a life coach—she's your guide to unlocking your fullest potential. With a passion for personal growth and development, Jennifer is a sought-after speaker, captivating audiences with engaging talks and workshops that inspire transformation. As a seasoned MC/host, she adds a touch of warmth and charisma to weddings, ensuring unforgettable moments for couples and guests alike.

She serves as a Notary Public and is an active member of the Kingdom Life Church. She is married to Gary and has four sons, one daughter-in-love, and two granddaughters.